KHALID AND KHALILAH'S ABC'S OF BLACK HISTORY

DR. KHALID EL-HAKIM

FIRST EDITION 2021

Muhammad Ali (Cassius Clay) was born in Louisville, Kentucky on January 17, 1942. Ali started boxing at the age of 12. He won his first Golden Gloves award at 15 and a gold medal in the 1960 Olympics when he was 18. Muhammad Ali is considered by many to be the greatest boxer ever. He won 56 fights out of 61. In 1967, he refused to be drafted into the Vietnam War, and his title was taken from him. Ali used his popularity to uplift Black people and the rest of humanity. He was a hero to people all over the world. The Muhammad Ali Center in Louisville, Kentucky opened on November 19, 2005 and displays thousands of artifacts that celebrate his exceptional life.

A
is for
Muhammad ALI

I AM the Greatest!

Octavia Butler was born in Pasadena, California on June 22, 1947. Octavia started writing when she was 10 years old and never let the challenges of dyslexia hinder her love of reading. Science fiction was a way Octavia was able to escape the stresses of life. Her most popular book, Kindred, sold over 450,000 copies. In 2015, Adrienne Maree Brown and Walidah Imarisha co-edited Octavia's Brood: Science Fiction Stories which is a collection of 20 short stories and essays inspired by Butler. She won many literary awards including a MacArthur Fellowship in 2000.

B
is for
Octavia BUTLER

Embrace difference.

Shirley Chisholm was born in Brooklyn, New York on November 30, 1924. She spent part of her childhood in Barbados living with her grandmother who told her that she was going to be someone special. In 1964, Chisholm was elected to the New York State Assembly. She became the first Black woman to be elected to Congress in 1968 and served seven terms. In 1972, she became the first woman to run for president under a major party. In 1983, Chisholm retired from Congress and began teaching at Mt. Holyoke College. She was awarded the Presidential Medal of Freedom in 2015. Vice President Kamala Harris credits Chisholm for being an inspiration to her to enter politics.

C

is for

Shirley CHISHOLM

We want our fair share now!

Dr. Angela Davis was born in Birmingham, Alabama on January 26, 1944. As a little girl, she was very involved in the Girl Scouts which gave her an early experience in community service. She was an exceptional student and went to Brandeis University on a scholarship. Early on as an activist, Dr. Davis was a member of the Black Panther Party, SNCC, and the Communist Party. Today, Dr. Davis is an internationally known lecturer on women's rights and criminal justice reform. She is the author of over 20 books and was included in Time Magazine's 100 Most Influential People of 2020.

D
is for
Dr. Angela DAVIS

Being Black ensures there will be struggle.

Duke Ellington was born on April 29, 1899 in Washington, D.C. Duke loved music from an early age. He began playing piano at the age of seven after listening to his mother play. Duke Ellington had a career as a band leader and composer that spanned over six decades. Some of his most famous songs are Take the "A" Train, Satin Doll, and It Don't Mean a Thing. He won many awards including a Grammy Lifetime Achievement Award, Presidential Medal of Honor, and Pulitzer Prize. Duke Ellington is considered a national treasure and is one of the most influential musicians in Jazz history.

E

is for

Duke ELLINGTON

A problem is a chance for you to do your best.

Aretha Franklin was born in Memphis, Tennessee on March 25, 1942. She is known throughout the world as the Queen of Soul. Aretha's father recognized her talent at a young age when she used to sing in the church choir in Detroit, Michigan. She recorded her first songs at the age of 14. Aretha went on to become one of the most influential singers in history. She recorded 48 albums inspiring singers in a variety of different musical backgrounds such as gospel, rock, R&B, jazz, soul, and hip hop. She was nominated for 44 Grammy Awards and won 18. Among many other notable awards, she was honored by President Obama with the Presidential Medal of Freedom.

F

is for

Aretha FRANKLIN

Women absolutely deserve respect.

Marcus Garvey was born in Saint Ann's Bay, Jamaica on August 17, 1887. As a child, Garvey had a love for reading. He left school to become a printer's apprentice where he led a strike for higher wages. In 1924, he founded the Universal Negro Improvement Association (UNIA) in Jamaica and then moved to Harlem, New York where the organization thrived. He taught Black people to love themselves and that Africans should be united all around the world. He is considered Jamaica's first national hero and his image is on Jamaica's 25 cents coin. Marcus Garvey's Red, Black and Green flag is one of his many lasting legacies.

G

is for

Marcus GARVEY

UNIA

Up you mighty race. Accomplish what you will.

Kamala Harris was born in Oakland, California on October 20, 1964. Early in life, Kamala experienced growing up in a racially divided country when she was bused to an all white school in Berkeley, CA. Her parents divorced when she was seven. When she went to visit her father on the weekends, white children in the neighborhood were not allowed to play with Kamala and her sister because they were Black. Being treated unfairly did not stop her from being successful. Kamala grew up to become the first Black woman Attorney General of California. She also served as a Senator in Congress and was the first Black and Asian woman elected as Vice President of the United States of America in 2020.

H

is for
Kamala HARRIS

Vice President

You are powerful and your voice matters.

Ice Cube (O'Shea Jackson) was born on June 15, 1969 in Los Angeles, CA. He had very strong and loving parents who sent him to a suburban school in San Fernando Valley to keep him out of trouble in the negative environment of South Central LA. Cube began writing raps in high school and eventually combined his talents with other artists, forming the hip hop group NWA. With his success as a rapper, he also became an actor and director. One of his most popular family movies is Are We There Yet? In 2017, Ice Cube was honored with a star on the Hollywood Walk of Fame. He has also received a BET Hip Hop Award, VH1 Hip Hop Honor, and Blockbuster Entertainment Award.

I
is for
ICE CUBE

Today was a good day!

Dr. Mae Jemison was born on October 17, 1956 in Decatur, Alabama, but she grew up in Chicago. Dr. Jemison knew at a young age that she wanted to be a scientist and astronaut. As a college student at Stanford, she studied medicine. After graduating, she served in the Peace Corps and then decided on a career in engineering. In 1987, she was accepted into NASA's space program becoming the first Black woman to travel into space. She spent 8 days orbiting the earth in 1992. Among many honors, Dr. Jemison is in the National Women's Hall of Fame and the International Space Hall of Fame.

J
is for
Dr. Mae JEMISON

I always knew I'd go to space.

Dr. Martin Luther King, Jr. was born in Atlanta, Georgia on January 15, 1929. At the age of 13, Dr. King won a speech contest showing his early skills as a speaker with an impressive voice. At the age of 15, he enrolled at Morehouse College and graduated at the age of 19. Dr. Martin Luther King, Jr. became one of the most important figures in history for the cause of social justice and human rights. He led the March on Washington on August 23, 1963 where he delivered his famous "I Have a Dream" speech. In 1964, Dr. King won a Nobel Peace Prize for his commitment to confront racism through non-violent direct action. He is honored every year on MLK Day, a national holiday celebrated on the 3rd Monday in January.

K
is for
Dr. Martin Luther KING, Jr

I've been to the mountain top!

Jacob Lawrence was born on September 17, 1917 in Atlantic City, New Jersey. His mother enrolled him in art classes in Harlem, New York to keep him busy as a child. Using crayons, he used to copy the patterns on his mother's carpet. Jacob taught at the University of Washington and his most noted work is called the Great Migration. He received many awards including the Spingarn Medal by the NAACP, U.S. National Medal of Arts, Algur H. Meadows Award for Excellence, and The Washington Medal of Merit. He received honorary degrees from Harvard, Yale, Howard, and New York University.

L

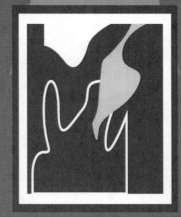

is for

Jacob LAWRENCE

You bring to a painting your own experience.

Oscar Micheaux was born on January 2, 1884 in Metropolis, Illinois. As a young man, Oscar had a variety of jobs including traveling the country as a Pullman Porter on trains. Traveling opened up his world to different experiences which he incorporated into his writing and films. He wrote seven novels and made 40 films. In 1919, his film The Homesteader was shown in theaters around the country. Micheaux has been acknowledged for his contribution to the film industry with a star on the Hollywood Walk of Fame. He also received an award from the Directors Guild of America and is featured on a U.S. Postal Stamp.

M
is for
Oscar MICHEAUX

I use my films to elevate the colored race.

Dr. Huey P. Newton was born on February 17, 1942 in Monroe, Louisiana. His family moved to Oakland, California while he was a child. In college, Huey became an activist and organized a group of youth to protect the community from police brutality. He and co-founder Bobby Seale, named their group The Black Panther Party for Self-Defense. The Black Panthers started several community based programs including the Free Breakfast for Children Program, a free clinic, and the Oakland Community School. The Black Panther Party grew as an organization across the country with hundreds of chapters. Dr. Huey P. Newton earned his Ph.D. from the University of California in 1980.

N

is for

Dr. Huey P NEWTON

Power to the People!

Barack Hussein Obama II was born on August 4, 1961 in Honolulu, Hawaii. Growing up, Obama lived in culturally diverse communities in Hawaii and Indonesia. Those experiences helped shape his worldview and inspired him to pursue a degree in political science with a specialty in international relations at Columbia University. He became a community organizer in Chicago after graduating from Harvard with a law degree. He set his sights on politics in Illinois and was elected to the U.S. Senate in 1997, serving three terms. Setting his political goals even higher, Obama was the first Black person elected as President of the United States in 2008, serving two terms in office.

Gordon Parks was born in Fort Scott, Kansas on November 30, 1912. A white teacher discouraged Parks from going to college saying, "It would be a waste of money." He picked up a camera when he was 25, taught himself how to take photographs and it changed his life forever. As the first Black photographer for Vogue and Life magazines, Parks shot iconic photos of Black life in America. Besides photography, Parks was a accomplished musician, author, and filmmaker. In 1971, his overwhelmingly successful film Shaft was released. Parks has received many national and international awards including a Living Legend Award from the Library of Congress.

P

is for
Gordon PARKS

Photography was my choice of weapons.

Queen Latifah (Dana Owens) was born in Newark, New Jersey on March 18, 1970. She played basketball in high school and performed in the musical The Wiz in a school play. She started out as a beatboxer for a group called Ladies First, but eventually found her voice as a solo artist. In 1989, Latifah signed to Tommy Boy Records, setting a new standard on how women were represented in the male dominated culture of hip hop. Her hits include U.N.I.T.Y. and Ladies First. In addition to hip hop, Queen Latifah is a singer and actor. She was the first female hip hop artist to be nominated for an Oscar and the first hip hip Cover Girl model.

Q

is for
QUEEN LATIFAH

Ladies First!

Wilma Rudolph was born in San Bethlehem, Tennessee on June 23, 1940. When Wilma was five years old she had to wear a leg brace because she suffered from polio and other childhood illnesses. She played basketball and ran track in high school. While a junior in high school, Rudolph competed in the 1956 Summer Olympics. In 1960, she won three gold medals and broke three world records in the Olympics in Rome. Rudolph became the first American woman to win three gold medals in track and field in the same Olympic game. In 1983, she was inducted in the U.S. Olympic Hall of Fame.

R

is for

Wilma RUDOLPH

Freedom is never given; it is won.

Arturo Schomburg was born on January 24, 1874 in Santurce, San Juan, Puerto Rico. When Schomburg was in grade school, one of his teachers told him Black people never made any important contributions to history and have no heroes. Schomburg did not accept that as truth. So, he dedicated his life to researching, writing, and teaching the historical contributions of Black people. He also collected literature, art, and other artifacts reflecting untold stories of a people who were written out of history. Today, the Schomburg Center for Research in Black Culture in Harlem now bears his name with more than 11 million items in its archives.

S

is for

Arturo SCHOMBURG

The American Negro must remake his past in order to make his future.

Sojourner Truth was born into the horrible condition of slavery around 1797. At the age of nine, she was sold at auction with a flock of sheep for $100. She was sold several more times until she escaped to freedom with her infant child. Sojourner Truth changed her name from Isabella Baumfree after hearing "the Spirit of God calling her to preach the truth." As an abolitionist, she traveled the country lecturing against the evils of slavery and for women's rights. She delivered her most famous speech, "Ain't I A Woman", in 1851 at the Ohio Women's Rights Convention in Akron, Ohio.

Blair Underwood was born on August 25, 1964 in Tacoma, Washington. Blair's father was in the military so he spent his youth living on army bases in America and Stuttgart, Germany. He attended high school in Virginia and studied at the Carnegie Mellon School of Drama. Blair's acting debut was in the classic hip hop film, Krush Groove. He has enjoyed a long and successful career in Hollywood, appearing in 40 movies and 29 television shows. Underwood has received many honors over the years for his contributions to the entertainment industry including six NAACP Image Awards and a Grammy Award.

U
is for
Blair UNDERWOOD

To still be standing 20 years in this business is a great feeling.

James VanDerZee was born on June 29, 1886 in Lenox, Massachusetts. He bought his first camera when he was a teenager and made a darkroom in his parent's home in Harlem, New York. In the 1920's and 1930's, he took hundreds of photographs of Harlemites. Many of his subjects included famous people such as Bill "Bojangles" Robinson, Countee Cullen, Joe Louis, and Marcus Garvey. His photographs are highly collectible today, some are valued thousands of dollars for a single photo. He gained international fame in the art world when his photography was featured at the Metropolitan Museum of Art in 1969.

V

is for

James VANDERZEE

Happiness is perfume, you can't pour it on somebody else without getting a few drops on yourself.

Madam C.J. Walker was born on December 23, 1867 in Delta, Louisiana. At the age of 14, she escaped abusive work conditions and mistreatment from her brother-in-law. In the 1890's, she began developing and experimenting with hair care products after suffering from hair loss. Experiencing success with her own hair, she began selling her products around the country, and trained women using her "Walker Method". As her profits grew, she opened factories and employed women around the country to sell her products. She is known for being the first self-made woman millionaire in America.

W

is for

Madam CJ WALKER

I got my start by giving myself a start.

Malcolm X (Malcolm Little) was born on May 19, 1925 in Omaha, Nebraska. When Malcolm attended high school in Michigan, a white teacher crushed his dream of becoming a lawyer by declaring law was not a realistic career for a Black person. He dropped out of school and became involved in a life of crime. In 1945, he was sent to prison. While in prison, he was introduced and accepted the teachings of The Honorable Elijah Muhammad's Nation of Islam. He soon became the national spokesperson for the organization, preaching about Black pride and self-determination. The Autobiography of Malcolm X details his fascinating life of transformation and has inspired millions of people around the world.

X

is for

Malcolm X

"THE FUTURE BELONGS TO THOSE WHO PREPARE FOR IT TODAY".

A man who stands for nothing will fall for anything.

Coleman Young was born on May 24, 1918 in Tuscaloosa, Alabama. Young moved to Detroit, Michigan with his family in 1935 and graduated from Eastern High School. He worked for the Ford Motor Company and the U.S. Postal Service. Prior to becoming a politician, he was a Tuskegee Airman serving as a second lieutenant and navigator. In 1964, he was elected to the Michigan State Senate. In 1973, he was the first Black person elected as mayor of Detroit and served five terms. He was known for being a fighter and protector of the citizens of Detroit. He was awarded the Spingarn Medal from the NAACP in 1981.

Y

is for

Coleman YOUNG

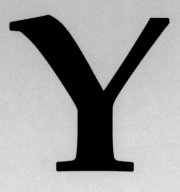

WELCOME To DETROIT

Courage is one stop ahead of fear.

Zora Neale Hurston was born on January 7, 1891 in Notasulga, Alabama. When she was three, her family moved to the all Black town of Eatonville, Florida. She credits school teachers who gifted her books for sparking her love for reading. In 1924, she graduated from Howard University and then attended Barnard College where she was the only Black student. She wrote more than 50 short stories, essays, and plays. In 1937, her most popular novel, Their Eyes Were Watching God, was published. In addition to being a writer, she was an anthropologist and filmmaker.

Z

is for

ZORA Neale Hurston

Love, I find, is just like singing.

Made in the USA
Monee, IL
14 June 2021